Little Miss Muffet

Ian Beck

OXFORD

OXFORD

UNIVERSITY PRESS

Great Clarendon Street, Oxford OX2 6DP

Oxford University Press is a department of the University of Oxford.
It furthers the University's objective of excellence in research, scholarship,
and education by publishing worldwide in

Oxford New York

Athens Auckland Bangkok Bogotá Buenos Aires Calcutta
Cape Town Chennai Dar es Salaam Delhi Florence Hong Kong Istanbul
Karachi Kuala Lumpur Madrid Melbourne Mexico City Mumbai
Nairobi Paris São Paulo Singapore Taipei Tokyo Toronto Warsaw

with associated companies in Berlin Ibadan

Oxford is a registered trade mark of Oxford University Press
in the UK and in certain other countries

First published 1988
Reprinted 1988, 1989
First published in paperback 1989
New edition published 2000

British Library Cataloguing in Publication Data available

ISBN 0-19-272390-1 (paperback)
ISBN 0-19-279050-1 (hardback)

Printed in Hong Kong

Beck, Ian

Little Miss
Muffet

JP

1780737

Little Miss Muffet sat on a tuffet,
Eating her curds and whey,
When along came a spider,
Which sat down beside her,
And frightened Miss Muffet away . . ?

Little Miss Muffet sat on a tuffet,
eating her curds and whey,

When along came . . .

. . . the Sun, bringing hours of fun,

'You'll need me to brighten your play.'

Then along came . . .

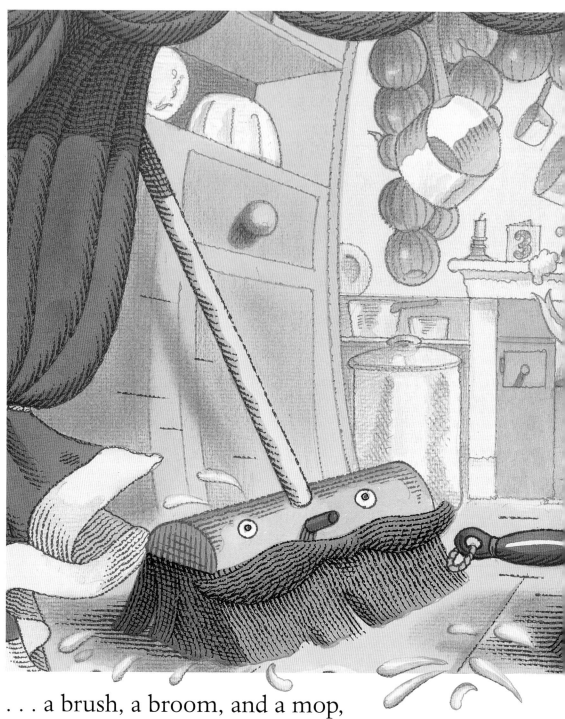

. . . a brush, a broom, and a mop,
all cleaning away, they just couldn't stop.

'We'll sweep you up too, if you stay!'

Then along came . . .

. . . four mice, who weren't very nice,

'We're Sneaky, and Slinky, and Shifty, and Stinky,
and we'll steal all your goodies away.'

Then along came . . .

. . . a cat, both fat and aloof,
  who spent all his time alone on the roof.

'I eat up six mice every day.'

Then along came . . .

. . . the marvellous, magical Moon,
who brought all the stars in her silver balloon.

'Make a wish if a star falls your way.'

Then along came . . .

. . . Freddy the Fantastic Frog,
with Yip-Yip-grr-Bow-Wow the Vanishing Dog.

'Allez-oop-through-ze-'oop and olé!'

Then along came . . .

. . . a clown, from the circus in town,
he juggled some pies full of custard surprise,
and then with a 'splat' he sat down.

'Watch out! There's one coming your way!'

Then along came . . .

. . . a 'Thing' in a box tied with string.

'I'll stay inside here if I may.'

Then along came a spi . . .

. . . spindly, spangly witch,
high up on her broom, with a cat black as pitch.

'You'd better not get in my way.'

Then along came a spi . . .

. . . spiteful and horrid old croc,
who kept something nasty wrapped up in a sock.

Then along came a . . .
Great big, Hairy, Fat, Spi . . .

. . . Spider! – who sat
down beside her!

BUT! . . .

. . . the Sun, the brush,
the mop, and the broom,
the mice, and the cat,
and the silvery Moon,
   the fantastic frog,
   and Yip-Yip the dog,
the clown from the town,
and the 'thing' tied with string,
the spangly witch
with her cat black as pitch,
and the awful old croc
with his terrible sock,
and mainly Miss Muffet,
I'm happy to say . . .

all frightened, all frightened,
all frightened, all frightened,

they frightened the spider away . . .

Hooray!